T0244905

ACCIDENTS

Genni Gunn

EDITIONS

Cover art "Pattern Distraction" by Marven Donati.
Cover design by Doowah Design.
Photo of Genni Gunn by Tom Hawkins.

This book was printed on Ancient Forest Friendly paper.
Printed and bound in Canada by Hignell Printing Inc.

We acknowledge the support of The Canada Council for the Arts and the Manitoba Arts Council for our publishing program.

Library and Archives Canada Cataloguing in Publication

Title: Accidents / Genni Gunn.
Names: Gunn, Genni, author.
Description: Poems.
Identifiers: Canadiana 20220164177 |
ISBN 9781773240985 (softcover)
Classification: LCC PS8563.U572 A73 2022 |
DDC C811/.54—dc22

Signature Editions
P.O. Box 206, RPO Corydon, Winnipeg, Manitoba, R3M 3S7
www.signature-editions.com

for Verbena

TABLE OF CONTENTS

ABSENCES

ARTIFACTS

ACCIDENTS

ABSENCES

Quarrels

Abandoned, a cupboard of mismatched plates
begun like us, as sets of four, but dwindled
when my mother's ire exploded
and Father smashed his plate on the floor.

How many encores are enough before we can agree
to leave enough alone? I should have smashed mine too
her echoes in my head: *You're sneaky and not to be trusted.*
Don't tell secrets to girlfriends or they'll betray you.
Why do you lock your diary? When I was your age, I was innocent.

We would have needed dozens sets of earthenware
to scrub away the words. Beneath the surface
mantle currents undulate, move plates
inside the earth, this liquid rage
a perfect storm, motion and heat.

We could have kept a tally of our conflicts
by the absences, files of cold cases
or photos of the missing on a wall
in need of understanding, for it's the knowing
that joins us to the ghost limbs of our past
those ruptured, beating hearts.

Secrets

Mysterious shapes, with wands of joy and pain,
Which seize us unaware in helpless sleep,
And lead us to the houses where we keep
Our secrets hid, well barred by every chain
—Helen Hunt Jackson

Our houses brimmed
with secrets; disguised
they showed themselves
and still remained unseen
sly serpents we glimpsed
from the corners of our eyes
in the swift intake of our breaths.
They slithered into corners
under commodes, couches, beds
mysterious shapes, with wands of joy and pain.

No one pretended they did not exist.
Rather, we all trod carefully
afraid to startle them and force
out loud futile, dangerous
discoveries. The threat, however
loomed: we might have fingered one
coiled inside a drawer, looped in a shoe box
tangled in a mat beside the bed.
In daylight, we avoided all dark spaces
which seized us unaware in helpless sleep

and talked of nothing that remained unshared.
At times, a secret would rear up
tongue lashing at our faces
following the *pungis* of our fears, the why
and where our parents roved
the words *abandonment* and *home*.
But, timid, we retreated
and still retreat today,
surprised to find those secrets live
and lead us to the houses where we keep

ourselves in order, where we keep
at bay those childhood memories that maim
for life. Yet we are still on edge
the precipice of knowing too steep.
The skins we wear, too delicate
too frail to leave behind. Today I ask
myself: do we still thwart the truth
keep mysteries in place or are
our bodies dwellings where
our secrets hid, well barred by every chain?

Trieste

1. Father

This is the city where my father's ghost
paces the port, the shimmering sea
ablaze with sails, with memory's scales
imbalanced, that shudder in the Bora's breath
in shops, outdoor cafés, through urban myths
between the columns of a church; the echo of his voice

in the evening dusk, elusive white noise;
I seek his face in the Grand Canal, the restless ghost
the blindfold, balance, sword, the myth
of justice, follow the narrow path above the sea
to the crack of bullets and batons, where the breadth
of hate erupts, crosses oceans and continents, scales

mountains, navigates rivers, rides rails
and my father, dead, unvoiced
not in a *Dulce et Decorum Est*
fantasy, but back home, across the bay where ghosts
of blue orange cranes in wingless flight foresee
Canadian haze. Exile. Around the heart a myth

of prowling gusts howling, like ones that beasts emit
in labyrinths and caves, the hollow depths and scales
of life, the Carso prison by the sea.
What secrets did he cage, what voice
that they could carve and chisel ghosts
turn hearts to scaffolds? What mournful breaths

fill runnel, flute and shaft? Each night, his breath
rattles the windows; curtains shudder; what skit
is this? Restless cracks cross my walls, the ghost
father of my youth returns in a gale
of images and cadences men murmur as they pass, the voices
of Trieste, my native home, the lulling of the sea

but it's enough I'm witness, my father free
from fragments of his life, his death
still fresh; no archived voice
nor print can solve the myth
he is. It's up to me now to scale
the bluffs of time, to scour our familiar coasts

Vancouver port, Trieste, to chase his ghost
down childhood trails
that lead me here, breathless and too late

2. Barcolana Regatta

It always saddens me to see the break
down after the party, the weeks
of preparations, the mounting swell
of masts and sails, the jostling in the bay
anticipation for the race, the boredom
of the last few hours, the wait. And then it's over
my father's life, a quick dismantling of all
that seemed so permanent
the striped concessions' shells ripped off
exposing frames worn and insubstantial

Behind the scenes, on backstreet trucks
men work unseen their faces bent
to the darkening sky their hands
tear at the limbs of popup tents
and haul them into crates

In an alcove in the emptying piazza
a Venus glimmers in the dark

3. Trieste Centrale

How often did you ride these trains
and pause on platforms   false starts
and stops   how many borders crossed
and you a kite in flight
away from us yet bound

Stations flit past like memories
confined   swivelling on state
lines   the ribs of steel
and stone   you hovering on
the threshold of our lives

Inside an archive a half century later
Your gaze unflinching
from a theatre of war   a theatre
of regrets   newsprint brittle
your uniform a disguise

These platforms where I pause
to board or leave behind
this journey on recurrent rails
homecoming or only steel extended
between home and home and home.

Ancestral Home

> *My parents rise out of their thrones*
> *into the milky rooms of clouds. How can I sing?*
> *Time tells me what I am. I change and I am the same.*
> *I empty myself of my life and my life remains.*
> —Mark Strand

Udine dwindles to fields
vineyards, cattle grazing, agritourism
I trace a road to our ancestral home
Pozzecco a serpentine memory
of country lanes, silkworms and English words
I wanted to be Canadian even then
In the apartment to the right
my parents rise out of their thrones

and flee on chariots of longing. That summer
the great-aunts braided my hair with mottled hands
seduced me with tales of unrequited love
their creased and folded faces
their spines curved under
the burden of two world wars
they forced my English
into the milky rooms of clouds. How could I sing

when no one was listening?
Upstairs in seven bedrooms
grandparents, aunts and uncles
conceived children, argued, made up, cried
sewed curtains and quilts
built boats in bottles, fought wars and died
Their portraits stared from the walls
as if awaiting repossession
guarding memory and history
their ghost eyes followed me
hurling accusations in Furlan
time tells me what I am. I change and I am the same

child staring at the mausoleum walls
night jasmine and honeysuckle scents
the valance on the windows
sun-faded roses of another era
I don't belong to strangers now live
inside this home I view on Google maps
I leave behind this past of stinging tentacles
and translucent sea anemones
I empty myself of my life and my life remains.

Landfill

Hairline cracks begin along the tiles
of my mother's house
pining for exposure perhaps
crow's feet on snow, around the eyes
atlas roads that crack and heave
craters flinging up the ashes of a life
memories fallen like tailings in a pond
the water bloody, still, the foamy orange swells
an artist's rendering of calm
a toxic lifelong crevasse
her living room slumps into

Yes, it can be repaired
tiles ripped out, concrete smashed
inside the hollow she lies
and listens to the gravel drone
a landslide that takes her breath away
till she is landfill sinking

Aftermath

She bought an easel, a roll of canvas, acrylics whose names
Cerulean Blue, Morocco, Sienna, Blood, Cyan, and Alcatraz
could transport her to outlandish places. She stretched the canvas
around as many wooden frames as she had colours, and began to
paint.

With Morocco, she painted square boxes with holes for windows
through which the canvas showed, because she had done no
underpainting. The effect of this happy oversight allowed a
brilliant sun to bleed through those holes—the unbleached canvas
dotted with blemishes in various hues, like sun spots appear in
front of the eye when staring too long at a bright light.

This catapulted her into an operating room, the surreal, wide-
angle faces of doctors peering from above, their jowls loose and
folded, frowning, from what she now imagined must be the
equivalent of heaven. She began a new canvas, and not wanting
to recall the operating room or her doctors, she painted the entire
canvas Cerulean Blue and left elongated head-holes for people
and for those blinding lights. So again, the effect was a happy
accident of brilliant sun in a summer sky.

She continued like this, painting each canvas a different colour,
but each painting betrayed her and, no matter what her intent
was, all she could see was bleached sun trying to come into her
room through the holes, the windows, the spaces she left open.

Frustrated, she kicked one of the tiny windows in Morocco.
Her foot went through and she found herself on a sunny beach,
without sunblock, surrounded by startling expressions of joy.

Crossroads

Awakened in the semi-dark
the house still, empty
the room a shadow tomb
her limbs tender, enflamed
by years, and rising from her bed
she gathers the unfulfilled

those arias, melodic trills
a yesterday of passion, love honed
razor-sharp, lovers fierce
nights filled with flood and fire
nerve endings raw unyielding

After her third husband died
she tried on a new self
reverted to the name her first spouse used
as if to resurrect his words
pry them from brittle pages
relive the choices, the arduous crossroads

the whys, the Y-junctions, forks taken or not,
the what-ifs, the if-onlys, the regrets
or maybe only the unknowable, the my-
stery, the might-have-
beens

But what if these divergences brought them
together? Each Y a destiny
we only discover generations later

Verbena's Paintings

In her paintings she is always naked
to the sharp flint stare
of viewers   her breasts and thighs pale
against a cacophony of colour, beneath the pattern
pieces of a past unstitched, the pencilled broken
line tracing the heart   the tissue cut

along the curvature of spine, a collage
of herself, edges left raw to the naked
eye. Inside her paintings she is always broken
limbs askew, face turned to the recurring lake—Narcissus stares
at her younger self, astonished that the widening pattern
of her albescent life has forged these pale

whitening concentric circles, this silence, the pigments pale
imitations of her hurried loves and lovers now cut
out. In the paintings she is always a pattern
of fury, of rage against rage, the brushstrokes harsh, her naked
hands trembling, child self, adolescent, basking inside the stare
of a man across a crowded room, and she unbroken

follows him home, a tenuous highway of broken
promises. In her paintings she is always a pale
shadow, a doppelgänger that men stare
at, the perfect mirror, the shortcut
to themselves. What they don't see is that her naked
flesh is thick and clotted with patterns

of her own design. The quills and scales, the patterned
carapace. Once she used words and touch like broken
glass. A tortuous highway, fields of naked
limbs against red roofs and blood-orange skies. Pale,
frail, in her paintings she is always cut-
and-paste, the extra on a movie set, going up stair-

wells. In her paintings, hers is a fixed stare
into primal chaos, time's abyss, her eyes patterned
by grief and disbelief   her body ripped and cut
and pasted bit by broken
bit onto the canvas, parchment pale
even the face naked

slate. Verbena, my mother, cut flower, a naked
blooming, the patterns pale
my stare unbroken

Mother

You are transparent now
muscles slack, the fist of your heart
exposed, ribs bent and bleached
a BodyWorlds exhibit come alive;
blood pulses through thick veins
of pain, of grief, through thick memory

layers, the lamina, the peel. What memories
lie bare and tender now?
What betrayal of a lifetime spent in vain
pursuits; so much concealing of the heart
with silks and wools and linens still alive
in spare-room closets, bleached

in the flare of happier days, bleached
like black-and-white memories
fading with each year. What makes us feel alive
in the days' quick gyre, an acceleration now
that adventures are a strain to start, the heart
struggling with the simple in-and-out, breath, veins

constricted, regrets sprouting like vervain
your namesake, the tears of Isis and Hera leached
into the present. What devil's bane, what flaming heart
what *cimaruta*, what sprigs of rue these branches of memory
a rose, a sword in hand, a fish, a crescent moon, a snake, an owl
a dolphin, cock, an eagle, the past revived

within these totems tattooed inside your name, and you alive
to your native Italy, fireflies in the pitch of night, weathervane
atop the roof, your father's webbed eyes, your mother's knit brows
Trieste a harbour teeming with ocean liners and sails bleached
in the albescence of memory
Atlantic waves, time's swirling eddies, your sweetheart

dead, all the homes abandoned, the hearths
the pianos termite-bored; yet you survived
your voids, concealed. Now honeycombs crumble; memories
swarm around you like nervine
remedies, scratching your lacquered overlays, breaching
the violent storm of age, the sorrow

the lifetime of self-deception. Fragile now
unmasked, I finally glimpse between bleached
ribs your heart in all its pulsing pain.

Absence

1.

It's the breath you don't hear, the pumping of the heart, the air between lips. On the phone, your mother's voice: an exhalation of loneliness. She names the inconsequential: who did what to whom, breakfast, lunch and dinner, visits to the doctor, to the store, to the fill-in-the-blanks, training sessions for the puppy whose love is boundless, this small creature who satisfies her yearning more than the daughters who live thousands of miles away, and who in youth pined for her, like the puppy, until that longing turned. Now it re-turns to its origin, the ache to please, to hold and be held, to feel her warm breath close, her voice, saying, "Yes."

2.

It's the music you recall at the oddest times. A jingle you heard that reminds you; a song you danced to at a high-school prom. How easy it is to sand off hard edges, forget the faces, remember only the small moments of desire. How music touched you. You were never the same, made yourself absent from home, a nomad across the country, arias in your brain, winding bass strings under your fingers, singing heartbreak, and at night, a vagabond under a wide expanse of sheets.

3.

It's the silence you hear when you flip through two decades of day-timers and agendas, time accelerating in reverse, exposing versions of yourself, paper thin, skin-deep, the dates and times of who-knows-what, names and shopping lists, phone numbers scribbled in the margins all reduced to mathematical equations. Inside those tidy squares are echoes of distant heartbreak, a dinner party, secrets whispered, the longing for what was, for all those who are missing now, their numbers useless.

ARTIFACTS

Masquerade

1.

The oldest from 9000 years ago
millennia of ritual, ceremonies
hunting, feasts, wars, performances
communion with the dead
protection from the plague
welders and gladiators
wear them, superheroes don them
for disguise, and riot police
raise them as shields

we blaze a trail of words
a historical / hysterical echo
a false face
a dark cloud before rain
a witch, a spectre
a buffoon

no wonder they're so maligned
ridiculed around the globe
today the unmasked
wear the shadow mask of death

2.

An eclipse is a mask
at GOP rallies under sweltering spotlights
everyone sports adoration, gold filigree
hammered over wood
their mouths open, lips spewing homage
to Dolus, that spirit of treachery
and guile, who tricked the gods
with lies   a mummery
the eclipse of reason

3.

Some mask their feelings
with lees of wine
lie and hide under
friendship's vermillion masks

some forge keyboard characters
emasculate themselves
pinned behind the bark
and leaves of anonymity

some nip and tuck their faces
as if this life were
a perpetual masquerade

4.

Burglars, Zorro, Robin Hood
Spiderman, Batman
dentists, doctors, nurses
skiers, football and hockey players
divers, catchers, fencers
carpenters, firefighters, armed forces
boiler men, painters, laboratory workers
Ku Klux Klan, Doctor Doom, Hannibal Lecter
Quattrocento Sicilians, Venetians, Brazilians
and all of us today

5.

The scold's bridle was a mask attached
to a locked iron muzzle studded with spikes
to dissuade women from speaking

yet words are masks too

6.

Unmasked, we'd be like newborns
abandoned to the wild
skin splayed to expose
the cloister of our ribs
and hermitage of the heart

conceal, veil, cloak, camouflage
shield, obscure, cover up, blind
disguise, pretext, facade

better to wear our plaster casts
these death masks that outlive us

Man Surprised by Death — Jan Punt 1758

a sheaf of wheat   the sickle   torch
and the man's arms raised against the blazing
years   as if he can ward off the skeleton
of all he's left undone   the splintered barn door
the milk jug leaning on a pedestal of bones

a rope   a bench   the brittle refuge
memory's boneyard   beneath a Roman church
the Crypt of Resurrection   a Lazarus tableau
of former friars   five-hundred years of skeletons
lustrous as tortoise shells   the nameless claiming

terra firma   years pass and dust reclaims
us all   in the cold dank underground of Rome
manifestos are coaxed into friezes   skulls and pelvises
ulnas and femurs   rib-flower rosettes   jawbone shields
startling visitors like me who stand at the recess

of our lives   oblivious to the manticore
its human head   its lion body aflame
porcupine quills   spines venomous   our skin
a thin disguise   collarbone eight-pointed stars
winged hourglass of shoulder blades   cadenzas

of warning   a scythe   a scale   crypts open doors
no one is spared   the reconstructed bones
the invitation   prepare
your vaults   weigh down the lids   monks are
bone chandeliers   how can one be surprised

What They Saved:
Reliquaries for Their Younger Selves

1. Butterfly

A hot theatre in the summer
and the lights are out
and the stars are out
and every night
she is transformed into a darkness
other than herself—Alma
an Egyptian dancing girl—
a magician's trick
the stage manager beads her
a false identity—a pink
butterfly to pin
flat in a case

2. Bottle

It resembles a Victorian poison flask
with ridged sides—a precaution
for the blind. This one
is made for languorous days
when cars drive by this gas station.
It's all about the price of premium
and customer suggestions
to make the boredom pass

Enter a girl from high school
she'd never known
or never tried to know
all that's not said in youth—the waste—
they face each other

Two red bulls on the bottle front
hooves pawing the ground
above a warning, or simply a reminder:
Call doctor for pregnant women.

3. Softball

And this is the Thunderheart
a mid-compression softball
that neither won a game
nor sailed out of the park
that no one signed
and no one wants

He stores it in a trunk
amid the remnants of his past

Thieves stole his other
prized possessions
his thunder heart, his trust
those trophies of a life well-risked

What he saves now is the evidence
of voids seldom filled

4. Puck

Black and shiny
made in Slovakia
How many miles has it slid on ice
from stick to stick
across lines
against boards
This is the puck the boy scored his first goal with
and, not allowed to keep it, flung it
into the stands, a slapshot into his cousin's
hands that clutched it all the way
out of the rink
and into the net
of his closet

5. Helmet

Dull moss green
could camouflage a soldier
in a mangrove swamp
or a highland forest
Inside, the emerald enamel gleams
olive cloth strap
and a blood-stained hatband
How can we understand Vietnam?
The tortured cries
throats slit
children dismembered
two men in a boat alone
with only their helmets.

6. Bulldog

What do you get from the Cloverdale Rodeo
if you've drunk too much
dust in your eyes, hay in your shoes
if you're tired of the clump of hooves
and the snort of pigs and the lowing of cows
What can you take from a Cloverdale Rodeo if not
a bulldog and a snake
to devour him?

7. Ring

A mother's love passed
through a heart-shaped ring
that winter in Bellingham
She is the diamond at the centre
recalled with every touch
a hard stone brilliance
carried from country to country
from bed to bed
this everlasting *love*
a grave mental disease.

8. Shoes

She loved walking in them
white leather, scuffed uppers, buckle and strap
slept in them fell in them wore them
even when she grew—in dreams, perhaps
If only we could remain inside our baby shoes
the world, a pristine mystery

9. Pointe Shoes

They sit on a shelf
coral with long satin ribbons
a pas de deux unfurling

once they danced every waking minute
from age three to fourteen
then a slip backstage
an accident—it's as easy as that—
the course of her life altered
only the pain remains
the glorious surrender to desire

10. Bracelet

She meets him after the darkest night
his face the glow of dawn
a pilot who flies through the northern lights

They speak in acronyms of faith
FROG she says (Fully Rely on God)
WWJD on the bracelet (What Would Jesus Do?)
and winds it round his wrist
and he replies PUSH (Pray Until Something Happens)

and wait for me.

11. Scrapbook

A first anniversary:
she searches everywhere for the perfect gift
makes him a scrapbook of their year together
He searches too
(she meanwhile has a manicure, just in case)
and hands her a scrapbook he's made.
See their faces, the momentary disappointment
They've been on and off for years
she turns a page and finds a letter
she'd sent him after a makeup
after a breakup
another letter—his declaration this time—
and she turns and finds him
hand in pocket
on his knees

12. Lion King

A bit pathetic, somewhat grotesque
yellowed fangs, orange fur
a green bug stuck under the pink tongue
he guards the door against no one

Once he was Lion King
plastic nostrils blasting fire
jowls open in a roar
ferocious and crouched with a boy
in the savannah bucket seats
of a Dodge Caravan

13. Book

Imagine a trek through bookstores
armed with money and a bag
large enough for *War and Peace*
the oxymoron title everyone
owns and few have read

Imagine five hours of this searching
books touched and thumbed through
first pages read and rejected
like nasty characters and bad politics
until there, on a shelf, a 1973 edition

It was summer and there was no *War
and Peace* in Langley,
only *Fear and Loathing
in Las Vegas*.

14. Lip Gloss

1003 shades of lip gloss shimmer
atop cosmetic counters

sparkly Vaseline to slip
and slide into
your pocket
when cameras roll
the mall is a continuous one-act play

customers stride in and out of
mistakes recorded as misdemeanours
and no one believes her

except her mother
and all of us
whose lips are parched
longing the gloss of truth

15. Tux

Her boyfriend is a T-shirt man
with heavy-metal riffs
no flowers, cellos or champagne
no frilly frocks on her

yet on her graduation night
he steps outside himself
into a suitable suitor in a suit
with a rose in his lapel

she hasn't met this man
before
or maybe
since

16. Owl

How often do people fall in love
with words other than their own?
She sends the author a full declaration
the seduction of his sentences
the allure of his allusions
the glamour of his grammar
the aesthetic of his assonance

Her idol sends her an alphabet
white, amber, black, brass beads
to spell her name
sends her a stuffed owl for power
one of his books in a foreign tongue

But she needs no translation
his words so universal
she loves this *Stranger
Than Fiction   Fight Club
Choke*
❤Chucky P

17. Photo

April in Barcelona
she recalls
a cramped hotel room overlooking the square
and two lovers below cinched in a passionate kiss
it was morning and they were dressed for work
a windmill turned in the square
the couple parted
their hands wistful, waved
over their shoulders
till they could no longer
see each other

18. Sketchbook

She keeps her twin sister's sketchbooks
years of them
her own too
decades from now
she'll discover herself
folded inside these pages
and recognize a house, a friend
two girls who died in a fire

ACCIDENTS

Accidents

It's been a year for accidents
crashes and heart attacks of various strains

revival is a possibility of miracles
and horrors, like marriage
an accident flimsy as the branch
a swimmer clings to in a flood

I am prone to accidents
knives lurch to slice me
scalding water bubbles my skin
ice cracks under my feet

my friend says
heart attack and *father*
and it's all too familiar
—distance, too, is an accident—
my own father taken years ago
and me miles away
my friend says
husbands and *wives*
love and *death*

those I have loved are
ghost limbs I preserve
in phone books and Christmas lists
unwilling to strike a line through
chapters of my life
these accidents—

the things we said or didn't say
the things we did or couldn't do—
I relive in slow motion
the headlights
the crush
the spin
of this divorce and that separation
and I wonder if or how
I could have swerved
to avoid the part
where the heart fails
over and over

Knowing

The blind cross streets to grasp your arms
board planes to sit beside you

When you stroll down a hall
white canes spill out of doorways

They tail you into movie theatres
greet you in parks restaurants and bars
ears attuned to the pitch of your voice
the weight of each foot against the earth

Sometimes in dreams
they navigate the arteries and tributaries
to your heart
chafed and familiar shores

In gardens they are nightshade burrs
clinging to your shirt

In oceans they are anemones
brushing your thighs

You cannot ignore them
or turn them away
they cleave to you—
lizards flattened against leaf or tree
heads tilted towards the sky
turreted eyes open and unseeing

They know you the way
refugees know one another

across a crowded room
the way in the dark
lovers trace concealed scars
the way a child
points to a missing limb
and asks where
and why
and how   do you survive
so blind
the blind need to lead you?

A Concise History
of Human Spontaneous Combustion

1.

Imagine for a moment Mount Stromboli
in the pit of your stomach; a flame

rising up the throat erupting in the air
above your head; imagine your lips

singed; your words turned
into incandescent heat; imagine ghosts

in 1654, outside the Copenhagen walls
drunkards lie, their mouths a firestorm

of brandy and vodka; their snores
an exhale of flames

demons scale ribs, soar from the gullet
Imagine the surprise, Dante's inferno, prayers.

2.

In France, a century later, Mme Millet airs
grievances in glass after glass, then smoulders on the floor

imploded into ash—what magic arts, what enflamed
passion, a tremolo of spurned

desire; in England, Grace Pett burns
to a heap of charcoal, her paper screen untouched.

A decade later still, in Italy, Countess Cornelia Bandi turns
to ash; her skull and stockinged legs intact, the blame

on baths of camphor, vanity, an ethereal ghost
Narcissus, beauty, the barbwire

of her thoughts, the whirlpools, the stumbling blocks.

3.

And so these stories grow into various myths:
alcohol saturation, electric sparks, boasts

of the heart, oxy-hydrogen gas, scorched love
phosphorus, mounds of fat, the air an irate

maelstrom of static electricity until in the early 1800s,
Guillaume Dupuytren debunks them all: a grassfire

of error. Alcohol, he says, makes one careless
with flames, matches, gas, illicit love affairs

clothes burn, ardour flickers and sputters, rage
sears lips. Reports cease, a century turns

to two. Impromptu human combustion extinguished.

4.

Then Saigon, 1963, a fermata rekindles the ghost
of self-immolation: Thích Quảng Đức lets bones and fire

speak. In pagan rituals, animals burned
in sacrifice to the gods. Imagine setting yourself aflame

imagine religious persecution, the words on your lips
a coda of wails and shouts, a flare

of extras clapping when Michael Jackson's hair
blazes through *Billie Jean* and Pepsi Cola videos, his ghostly

face, his white glove waves, his smile-wide lips.
What does he know of sacrifice, his head a gyre

of childhood longing, a moonwalk back through fame
on film. And later still

5.

the yearning of us all. Rebirth may be attained by fire
if you believe in afterlives; widows tied to funeral pyres

are not sweet singing birds; some women choose flames
over marriage ashes; dictators and politicians wage warfare

torch villages and countries; everyone fires guns, lightning strips
tree trunks, forests ignite, volcanoes churn

the earth a cauldron
ready to burst into spontaneous combustion.

Vietnam Journal, 2010

This paper, pen, ink
subtract one thing
the tree
a bridge over rapids
the fish spawning upstream
the bulrushes crushed
the riverbed flattened into an arid plain
where desert tortoises burrow
into rock shelters
in tunnels dug into the earth.
Subtract the place
where the tree fell
the deaths in its path
the underbrush choked
life subterranean now
trapped in a shaft
or scurrying like rats
in the Cu Chi tunnels
three storeys beneath
the earth. Young men's blood
lingering in the leaves

Inle Lake, Burma, 2006

It is the time when crimson stars/ Weary of heaven's cold delight,
And take, like petals from a rose, / Their soft and hesitating flight
Upon the cool wings of the air / Across the purple night.
—Ella Higginson

From the air, Heho is twilight on terra cotta roofs;
on the runway below red carpet furls to the tarmac's
edge, a crimson partition between soldiers
and the skeleton limbs of frangipani sheltering
ghosts and demons, army fatigues and AK-47s.
The generals are long gone to temples and gilded stupas
as if their presence could deceive the Buddhas
gold-foiling their way to paradise, and still they rage
division to division, state to state.
It is the time when crimson stars

score footprints in downcast eyes, in the furtive
turn of ankles on the street (downtown Vancouver
a military zone, dictators assembled in luxury suites
my city of hyphenated utopias—new-age, nuclear-free—
now hosting this party of dubious characters
and subduing protests in response with force). A fog descends.
We falter on the brim of cliffs, round hairpin curves, switchbacks
the mountainside exotic danger   *terra incognita*
and snake through the obsidian night
weary of heaven's cold delight

our blinded selves awakened to ethereal
apparitions in the shafts of light—
men, women, elusive, feet bare
longyis knotted at the waist, bicycle, trishaw, cart
drawn by water buffalo, smoke tinges the air.
Wordless, we step
into another century
where crepuscular ghosts
dissolve into shadows at the edge of the road
and take, like petals from a rose

our breaths, in the umbrage of mountains
phantoms and acacias scaffold the sky.
Then sporadic lights, the flicker between wooden slats
thatched huts, a guesthouse for foreigners like us.
In front of a crumbling façade, two men spring
from the shadows, sandals hollow on the wooden
planks where the pointed prow of a flat-bottomed boat
slaps a makeshift wharf, black-crowned
night-herons etch the horizon
their soft and hesitating flight

the only sound until the boatmen
squat at stern and bow and push
us off the wharf, until the splash of oars
the sweep of ironwood, our own
elated breaths, and in the dark
our pupils widen to contain the narrow
channel slashed between mist
and tall silhouettes of homes on stilts
night flowing beneath them
upon the cool wings of the air.

The motor sputters, we skim black
water, black night, the stars a dazzling net—
what a lure, this mystery unfolding
my heart fluttering, eyes and ears open
to the unknown, exhilarated by the wind
the spray of water at our sides
the brilliant sky and the darkness
enveloping us, like stepping through a tunnel
to emerge into a different world
across the purple night.

Fall

Rain   scattered memories   green chairs upended
in a gust   unwritten poems and letters
spool on the lawn like tumbleweeds
across time zones   my sister thrives in Burma
without autumns, her yellow hair
aglow in tropical suns, while here leaves fall
unhindered over everything, their yellow veins
industrious. I rake them
in my head while stories form, the blankets warm
around me   this bed a refuge
from what's undone, from words
unsaid now twisting in the air
these leaves of fall. The wind still
wails. Trees sag and branches sweep
the space between sky and sky
the penumbra of birds in flight. What darkening
this tug to face it all
to stand trembling at an open window.

Rangoon

In the elephant field
tall green ghost elephants
with your cargo of summer leaves
at night I heard you breathing at the window
—Jean Valentine

In my dreams, I am awakened by the polyphonic
whistle of a train, the rumble of monastery
prayers, the screech of crows, the tsk,
tsk, tsk of geckos, the croaks and squawks
of mynas—but mostly by dogs, always dogs
wild dogs howling, howling. They are the ghosts
of a forgotten land, the waking dead
who roam the marble steps of mansions
or straggle, famished,
in the elephant field.

Later, we drive the potholed
roads to the university grounds, tall
buildings slowly stifled by tentacles of vines—
a ghost town wild dogs own, ears cocked
for the sound of military boots. Beyond barbwire
nestled in grass, an armoured vehicle
targets the sky. A few kilometres past,
an open, thatch-roofed hut displays
glassware, and in a mound of dust
tall green ghost elephants

appear, through which I glimpse
a time when kings revered the rare
white beasts, before Than Shwe
and his military troops; the shackled

elephants are memories we carry
day to day, our wounds unhealed
they populate my dreams
trunks swinging in the dusty air.
Wild ghosts come closer
with your cargo of summer leaves

camouflage these wretched creatures
subdued under relentless sun
pacing the three short steps
to the end of their tethers. Listen—
the barking's closer now, wild, unrestrained;
next year these city streets will flow with monks
a futile blow the world shall hear;
for now, the restless ghosts
are hastening toward Naypidaw
at night I hear you breathing at the window.

Navigation

Late afternoon downtown Vancouver
the sun preens in the sheer glass of sky-
scrapers   turns lucent surfaces
to shields   the tenants safe   till dusk descends
and a flickering begins   one by one   windows blaze
a bank of screens migrating birds are drawn to
the masquerade of stars   how easily they navigate
toward a certain death

                              such languid inhibition
through open blinds   a crowd   strangers
sprawl on couches   slouch in chairs
their faces a harlequin of blues
eyes anchored by the flat elixir
of televisions   in rooms
above
                beside
                        below   lovers writhe
on a straight-backed chair   a woman strips
to a splintering heart   another lingers
inside the promise of a magazine   in the bedroom
blogs on a laptop LED   some stare
through telescopes   everyone
watching   as if awaiting

        Is all this the sum of perception
        an indifferent shrug of the inner eye
        gazing at the surface
        apathetic to the urgency of time?

and as the hours pass windows darken
one by one   we each recede
into the night   the birds are safe
for now   their flight assured
while I'm unbalanced
by our easy navigation

Temptation

It is an adventure much could be made of: a walk
on the shores of the darkest known river.
Among the hooded, shoving crowds, by steaming rocks
and rows of ruined huts half buried in the muck.
—Mark Strand

It begins with a smile
a door: interlocking teeth;
an expert at misinterpretation
you imagine yourself in every nuance of his lips.
The man presses into the small of your back
forward, forward, and the teeth open:
you close your eyes
it is an adventure much could be made of: a walk

into another flimsy love affair.
Eyes next, stairways you fall into
your feet heavier than marble
fall for the promise of breakfasts in bed
lazy orange mornings, the slow-motion run
giant sunflowers spiralling
on the shores of the darkest known

river. His hand presses down down
a shaft, fluorescent blue
sunlight, an orb diminishing
your breath comes quick, then you emerge
into the thick of black, cool wind
inside the earth
and you imagine the smell
of soot and sweat
among the hooded, shoving crowds, by steaming rocks

the sound of walls caving in
the feel of dust in the lungs.
Afterwards, he presses you
flat flat away from his cat and dog
wife, house, yard (fill in the clichés in any order)
away from I-love-you, we, forever
puts on his clothes and drives you
to the subway.
You'd think you'd learn.
Everyday living is a walk across an earthquake zone
a wade through baggage
and cremation remains
and rows of ruined huts half buried in the muck.

Love (aff)air, Aborted

ready for takeoff, an overnight flight
cabin dim, engines drone
they are quiet, seduced
by delicate FM melodies.
He fans around her
blades battering
a warning bell sounds and they begin
a countdown, intake, air rattles her ribs
blue lights red his breath in her hair.

In the distance a city twinkles in a Christmas
of yellow, purple, crimson
her house flashes the amber of an emergency
they are taxiing between zircon stars
between wet emerald blades
and the slick black onyx of asphalt.

Below, quadrant upon quadrant
points the solid black
of lovers awakened
her ears explode
depressurize the moment;
she forces air into her lungs
filtered through barren laughter.
She has survived this
and now retracts.

These Tears

> *To stare at nothing is to learn by heart*
> *what all of us will be swept into, and baring oneself*
> *to the wind is feeling the ungraspable somewhere close by*
> *Trees can sway or be still. Day or night can be what they wish.*
> —Mark Strand

After the shopping
lunch, dinner preparation
she slides in the CDs
—Beethoven symphonies—
the volume stirs up tears, so many
movements through rooms, houses, cities
babies, children, teens, adults
all afternoon she gazes out the window;
to stare at nothing is to learn by heart

our inner map, the arteries of yearning
the ventricles of pain
each journey, a swell of tears
all afternoon
she rearranges plants
furniture, dinnerware
each change, a new beginning/end
she fears the daily emptying
her lightness in the gusts of memory
what all of us will be swept into, and baring herself

to the lash of the past, welcomes
these tears—coiled snakes
music coaxes out
through the eyes
they slither down her cheeks
hissing secret binges
venomous whiskey breaths.
To hurl these sorrows
to the wind is feeling the ungraspable somewhere close by:

a scented white blossom of plumeria
a hummingbird in flight
an unraised voice, an unclenched fist
a silent evening, an unlocked door
a fearless night.
Weep, sweep, leap
it's all in the choice:
trees can sway or be still. Day or night can be what they wish.

Shaughnessy Ride

I'd like to chug and glide a train
up the rise into the gravity of Shaughnessy, angle
around the curves of Angus Drive, the slopes
of Lilliputian meadows the green of sky
feed ravens from an open window
and ride a CPR dome car into the past

before the concrete, the million-dollar frontages, past
memory's blockades. I'd like to ride a railway-baron train
lounge in a dining car and trace past curtained windows
the half-moon bays of Marguerite, angle
caboose past hedgerows, gaudy dancers, cedar sky
the luscious dips and slopes

of topiary beasts and yews that edge the slopes
I'd like to whistle-blow a locomotion past
gates and motion sensors, barrelling through sky-
blue pools and invisible fences, I'd like to steer a Cardinal train
through trespass laws and undulating angles
hands grasping willows weeping into ponds outside the window

elegant geometry, banks and arcs reflected in the window's
placid lake. I'd like to tumble down a lexiscape of slopes
the stagger joints and rock-offs, curl around angles
in degrees, on tangent tracks, steep gradients past
crossovers, turnouts and corridors of train
ghosts lingering in the terminal between earth and sky

pink magnolias, birds in flight, the stippled sky
a backdrop, marble and stone and shuttered windows
the air itself purified. I'd like to ram a train
through granite lives and porticos through market slopes
and slides down an embankment past
the manicured facades of Hosner, Nanton, Pine, angle

across sentinel displays, stacked railway ties angling
the landscape. Cargos' bandings rip into a guillotine sky
stakes drop, turnabouts cog past
spires and chimneys cupolas bay windows
columns and arches, wrought iron gates and copper slopes
of roofs. I'd like to tunnel-drive a train

metal on metal, the past a siding track, a train
angled into a cutting camellia sky
the screech of brakes the open window the violet slopes

Snow

Early December morning   the voice of winter
across shoal dreams   white muffled rage
on blades of grass   on sere hydrangea heads
hound's-tooth sky against the streetlight's yellow glow
It's a Wonderful Life   a chiaroscuro
happily-ever-after Hollywood
blizzard we shake from California lilacs   delicate weave
of branches shivering against white blades

and this goes on for days   a laminate of snow
blocking the drive   we abandon cars
chores   play indoor games   cancel appointments
A spade of change has chipped us
out of our adulthoods   trees shudder
and sudden shrieks barge
through the cracks in our inner skies
brittle   kaleidoscopic   shattered
into snowflakes
falling   night and day now weaving
themselves into the warp and weft of our replays
childhoods lost   the warp and weft of cedar hedges
the dampened crush of traffic on the street

What ark is this?   Our own desire the blade
that skates into the night   What if it never stops
the sky keeps falling   light dwindles and a hush
inhabits us   what if our house is overcome
trees slump across the drive   and we succumb to hollows
in the quilted snow   drift in the drift
sleet and ice   and this is not delay
but turning point?

In the Event

of an earthquake   stay calm   Avoid panic
If indoors crouch under desk or table   if outdoors
find an open space no trees   nothing to fall   Conceal
fear with vigour   Protect your temples
head and neck   Recoil from windows
After the shaking stops   expect aftershocks

when your lover departs   after the shock
wears off   your heart is a drained lagoon   a panic
attack   Keep curtains drawn   the windows
barred against the tidal wave   Outdoors
wind seethes   Stay calm   Erect a temple
in your head and wear a smile   Conceal

the blistering grief   In the event of fire   conceal
the burns and scars   Avoid the aftershocks
move to a Buddhist country   Gold leaf a temple
make rice   become a monk and never panic
despite the trucks of soldiers   Stay calm   Outdoors
walk barefoot   and when inside   open the windows

to welcome birds   cicadas   death   through windows
of your own design   a phoenix perhaps concealed
in a nest of boughs and spices   weary of its solitary life outdoors
what scarlet plumage in the heat of night   what aftershock
the pyre   gold-tinged feathers when the fire strikes   don't panic
collect the ashes in an egg of myrrh and take them to the temple

of the Egyptian god spend time in Heliopolis   a temple
to optimism   There's no alternative   only the fall from windows
a hundred storeys down   leaps into raging currents don't panic
a twist of rope   skid marks on a switchback road   sky congealed
in limbs of green   Stay calm   Lie in sun and welcome aftershocks
under your skin   Let grief surge through you   an outdoor

spring bound for the estuary   Stay calm   Move out of door-
ways into the light   Believe in miracles   build temples
in the air   beware the pyrotechnics   the aftershocks
new lovers   skin   voices that haunt you in the widowed
night   In the event of earthquakes   conceal
emotion in the desert of yourself   Stay calm   Don't panic

in the event of an event   impending death   build windows
to escape from   eternal arks   temples for disbelievers   to conceal
the aftershocks   bridges to span the sudden gulps   the panic

Acknowledgements and Notes

The following poems have appeared in the following magazines: "Snow," *Arc* (Winter 2017); "Accidents," *Contemporary Verse 2* (Spring 1998); "In the Event," *Event* (Winter 2018); "Shaughnessy Ride," *Vancouver VerseMap*, (Fall 2009); and "A Concise History of Human Spontaneous Combustion," *Discovering Voice (Italian Canadiana*, Volume 30, 2016).

In "Secrets," the four-line poetry excerpt is taken from "Dreams," by Helen Hunt Jackson (poets.org/poem/dreams-1).

In "Ancestral Home," "Temptation," and "These Tears," the four-line poetry excerpts are respectively taken from "The Remains," "Orpheus Alone," and "The Night, the Porch" by Mark Strand, from *New Selected Poems*, New York: Alfred A Knopf, 2007.

In "Inle Lake, Burma, 2006," the four-line poetry excerpt is taken from "Dream-Time," by Ella Higginson, from *When the Birds Go North Again*, London: Macmillan, 1898. Also, the lines "downtown Vancouver / a military zone" refer to the APEC conference, during which Pacific Rim leaders came together to discuss trade partnerships and economic development: "They were greeted by thousands of protesters rallying against what was then seen as the rise of neo-liberalism and the fall of democratic institutions—many were arrested and pepper sprayed... Even more worrisome was the fact that police had arrested protest leaders like student and anarchist activist Jaggi Singh in advance of the summit, telling them not to come back to campus"; quoted from Maryse Ziedler's CBC News article, "'We were at this tipping point': APEC protests at UBC continue to shape politics 20 years later." Posted on Nov 25, 2017 8:00 AM PT (www.cbc.ca/news/canada/british-columbia/we-were-at-this-tipping-point-apec-protests-at-ubc-continue-to-shape-politics-20-years-later-1.4417358). Last updated on November 25, 2017.

In "Rangoon," the four-line poetry excerpt is taken from "Ghost Elephants," by Jean Valentine, from *Break the Glass*, Port Townsend: Copper Canyon, 2012.

During the Covid-19 pandemic, like everyone else, I found myself at home for unlimited hours, during which I pondered this collection, added new poems, and completed this project that's been several years in the making. Much gratitude to John Barton — who also edited my last poetry collection, *Faceless*, fourteen years ago — for his insightful editing and even more, for his friendship and kinship. For her continued support and for her energy, humour and valued friendship, I want to thank Karen Haughian and Signature Editions. Last, but not least, I thank Frank for all the tangibles and intangibles.

About the Author

Genni Gunn, author, musician and translator, has published twelve previous books: three novels – *Solitaria, Tracing Iris* (which was made into the film *The Riverbank*) and *Thrice Upon a Time*; three story collections — *Permanent Tourists, Hungers* and *On the Road*; two poetry collections — *Faceless* and *Mating in Captivity*; a collection of personal essays — *Tracks: Journeys in Time and Place*; the opera libretto *Alternate Visions;* and three translations. Her books have been translated into Dutch and Italian, and have been finalists for major awards: *Solitaria* for the Giller Prize; *Thrice Upon a Time* for the Commonwealth Writers' Prize; *Mating in Captivity* for the Gerald Lampert Poetry Award; *Devour Me Too* for the John Glassco Translation Prize; and *Traveling in the Gait of a Fox* for the Premio Internazionale Diego Valeri for Literary Translation. Before she turned to writing full-time, Genni toured Canada extensively with a variety of bands. She currently lives in Vancouver.